Five First Rhyming Readers

by Annette Meredith

For Austin, Nina and Joe

With thanks to Michelle for her assistance
and to Ted for his ever-patient support and advice.
Thanks also to Dominic for the author photo, to Don Powers for the photo
of the magnificent hummingbird, to my brother Ian for the photo of the wheat field,
and to my friend Carol Thompson for building and photographing a snowman.

ISBN-13: 9781507875179
ISBN-10: 1507875177

Busy Bee

clover

honey bee

I think I see a busy bee,

Sitting on some clover,

flower

bee

Do you see a busy bee?

I think she's coming over!

bee on a flower

honey

honeycomb

Bees make honey from the flowers,
Sweet and oh so yummy!

bread and honey

May I have some honey please?
It would fill my tummy!

strawberry
patch

Flowers need the bees as well,

Bees aren't just for honey,

With no bees, there is no fruit,

And that is just not funny!

strawberries

cake

sunflower

So help the bees and grow some flowers,
Where it's nice and sunny,
Then the busy bees will come,
And soon there will be honey!

bye-bye, busy bee!

Hummingbird

Can you find a hummingbird,

Drinking from a flower?

Hummingbirds love nectar,

And drink it hour by hour.

hummingbird

If we give them something sweet,

We'll see them every day,

Until the end of summer,

When they all fly away.

They need to find a place that's warm,

And where there is no snow,

And so the little hummingbirds

Fly down to Mexico!

They like to come back in the spring,

Just as they did before,

And every year we say hello,

And welcome them once more!

two hummingbirds drinking nectar

bye-bye,
hummingbird!

Butterfly

butterfly

red flower

Hello little butterfly,

Here's a flower for you,

Do you like the pretty red,

Or will you find the blue?

blue flower

two butterflies

Your friends have found a pretty flower,
Its nectar is so sweet,

They drink the nectar all day long,
And never have to eat.

21

young caterpillar

older caterpillar

This caterpillar eats and eats,
Gets big, then eats some more,

And then it stops and has a rest,
Do you know what for?

the caterpillar is inside this chrysalis

chrysalis

A lot is going on inside,
And soon you will see why,

It's changing into something new –
A lovely butterfly!

bye-bye, butterfly!

Seasons

All the buds come out in spring,
Flowers bloom, birds like to sing.

spring

Warm sunshine and gentle rain
Make the flowers grow again.

Summer is a time for fun,
At the beach and in the sun.

summer

Bees are busy in the flowers,
We can stay outside for hours.

Autumn leaves come falling down,
Shades of yellow, red and brown.

autumn

Nuts and berries, corn and wheat,
Lots for everyone to eat.

Winter can bring snow and ice,
Sometimes it can be quite nice!

winter

When we tire of ice and rain,
Spring will soon be here again!

Spring again!

apple blossom

Little Seed

seeds and husks

bean seeds,
strawberry seeds
and sunflower seeds

Hello little baby seed,
You are very small indeed.

strawberry seeds

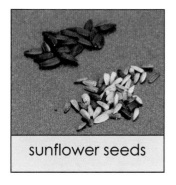
sunflower seeds

Let's see what you have inside,
Is there magic that you hide?

I will put you in a pot,
Then I hope it rains a lot.

acorns

oak tree

Even if you're very
small,
You can grow to be
so tall!

Are you a flower, are you a tree?
I just cannot wait to see!

Maybe you will make a treat,
Something good for us to eat.

melons

beans

Fruit or veggies, beans or peas,
You will hear us say "Yes, please!"

Words in this book

Core Words (some of the 100 most commonly used words):
the, be, is, are, to, of, and, a, in, that, have, has, I, it, for, not, on,
with, as, you, do, don't, at, this, by, from, they, we, say, she, or, will,
my, one, all, would, there, what, so, out, if, get, go, going, when,
make, can, like, time, no, just, know, year, your, good, some, them,
see, then, now, come, its, over, think, back, two, well, even, new, give,
day, us

Busy Bee

a, the, and, I, bee, see, you, be, so, on, do, she, oh, is, it, it's, my, as,
just, well, for, no, not, that, may, from, aren't, busy, funny, sunny,
think, have, fill, will, sitting, help, grow, need, make, come, coming,
some, honey, flower, sweet, clover, over, yummy, tummy, soon, please
where, would, nice, fruit; *honeycomb, bread, strawberry, patch, cake*

Words in italics appear only in the text boxes on the pictures

Hummingbird

a, the, and, you, we, we'll, them, they, to, see, of, from, it, by, if, all,
can, that, no, so, as, is, did, in, even, when, where, there, away,
find, fly, drink, drinking, give, love, need, like, come, say,
flower, hour, nectar, something, day, end, summer, hummingbird,
snow, place, Mexico, spring, welcome, warm, sweet, little,
just, before, every, year, hello, more, until, down, back, once; *two*

Butterfly

a, and, you, do, the, for, or, your, it, its, it's, is, so, they, all, have, to, this, has, what, for, lot, on, soon, will, see, why, into, new, then, hello, little, butterfly, here, flower, like, have, find, red, blue, big, friend, found, pretty, nectar, sweet, drink, day, long, never, get, eat, caterpillar, more, stops, rest, know, going, inside, changing, some, something, lovely; *two, young, older, chrysalis*

Seasons

a, the, and, in, to, for, all, out, is, it, we, are, at, of, be, lots, can, come, stay, bloom, like, sing, make, grow, eat, falling, will, bring, bud, spring, summer, autumn, winter, flower, bird, sunshine, rain, again, fun, sun, time, beach, bee, hour, leaves, shades, warm, gentle, busy, again, outside, yellow, red, brown, down, nut, berries, corn, wheat, here, everyone, ice, nice, snow, sometimes, quite, when, tire, soon

Little Seed

a, you, are, I, will, in, let, be, it, is, if, can, cannot, to, then, for, or, us, so, yes, pot, lot, very, hello, tall, small, little, good, there, that, what, inside, indeed, maybe, even, just, something, have, put, rain, hide, see, make, grow, hope, wait, hear, eat, say, baby, seed, magic, flower, tree, fruit, veggies, bean, pea, treat, please, strawberry; *husk, sunflower, acorn, oak, melon*

37

ABOUT THE AUTHOR

Annette Meredith is a master gardener, photographer and lifelong student of nature who is passionate about environmental issues and conservation. She was born in England but now lives in North Carolina, where she enjoys encouraging, observing and photographing nature as she works to improve sixty acres of woodland, meadows and organic gardens.
She also enjoys writing stories for children about birds, animals, insects, plants and wildlife that encourage young readers to learn about and appreciate nature.

If you have enjoyed this book, please leave an online review.
My primary goal is to inspire as many children as possible to learn about and understand the natural world around them. Your support would be greatly appreciated – thank you.

47278865R00024

Made in the USA
Charleston, SC
08 October 2015